Ink Splatters

JoyAnn

authorHOUSE®

AuthorHouse™
1663 Liberty Drive
Bloomington, IN 47403
www.authorhouse.com
Phone: 1-800-839-8640

First published by AuthorHouse   11/10/2011

ISBN: 978-1-4670-3923-9 (sc)
ISBN: 978-1-4670-3922-2 (hc)
ISBN: 978-1-4670-3921-5 (e)

Library of Congress Control Number: 2011917235

Printed in the United States of America

Contents

ABOUT THE AUTHOR

JoyAnn is a member of the epically proportioned Baby Boomer generation. She was born in New Orleans, Louisiana, during the early 1950s. Excluding the dislocation period created by Hurricane Katrina, during which she relocated to Arkansas, Joy is a permanent resident of New Orleans. She attended public schools there and later enrolled in night class where she received a GED. Afterward, she joined the Louisiana National Guard to help finance and continue her education. She next received a business degree from a local tech school (OIC) and attended Delgado Community College before transferring to the University of New Orleans (UNO).

After twenty years of military service, JoyAnn retired at the rank of sergeant first class (E7). She loves to write and spends many hours entertaining friends and family with letters, poems, and short stories. Joy has received recognition from numerous literary and playwriting contests. In fact, one of her entries was read at the Contemporary Arts Center in New Orleans. Terry Megan, a playwriting judge, commended Joy's strong writing abilities and meticulous sense of detail. In addition, Joy has participated in countless drama activities hosted by her hometown church, Beecher Memorial, UCC.

The author is currently a retired civil servant, a card carrying member of the AARP, and a religious affiliate of the community. After experiencing the turmoil and devastation of Hurricane Katrina, Joy wrote a book about her encounters, *In Search of Higher Grounds*. Her book is published through AuthorHouse (April 2009), ISBN 978-1-4389-2495-3.

Ink Splatters

JoyAnn

DEDICATION

This book is dedicated to the many who are overwrought by the increased destruction created by human error, natural disasters, or repeated acts of cruelty perpetrated by mankind upon each other. Where is the love? Tsunami, floods, earthquakes, forest fires, mud slides, tornadoes, hurricanes, hail storms, blizzards, etc.—some say we're in the last days. Murders, bullying, massacres, bigotry, mayhem, wars, hatred, ignorance, indifference ... we have abandoned Christianity. Repent ... truly repent ... for only He can save.

Others might conclude the world is on steroids. I say it is people and the environment that are haywire. The world—an inanimate sphere—appears to only be mirroring human drama and demonstrating the loss of its natural elements. Prayers, no doubt, hold our answers.

The events described herein are true interpretation as perceived by the author. Some incidents have been altered for clarity or omitted for brevity. In addition, character names have been omitted or changed to ensure privacy.

ACKNOWLEDGMENTS

I humbly acknowledge and appreciate the kindness of this nation as well as other countries that, during and after Hurricane Katrina opened their hearts and made available funds and housing to the Gulf Coast residents. Your support, charity, and outpouring of love were the elements required, and they provided the comfort desired. Christianity is a mighty cross, and there is room for everyone.

More specifically, I would like to thank US Army Retired General Russel L. Honore for his compassion and dedication throughout the mission of rescuing Katrina's victims. General Honore led a successful task force that alleviated insurmountable anguish experienced by many hurricane victims. While at the convention center, I'd been convinced that either no one cared or no one knew that we were trapped there. On my last day at the convention center, I caught a glimpse of this man. He was ordering troops to "shoulder their weapons." I don't know why the troops felt it necessary to hold their weapons in a defensive manner, but when the General showed up, he put a stop to that foolishness. Furthermore, when I got to Arkansas and had the opportunity to view Spike Lee's documentary, The Day The Levee Broke, *I was deeply moved by the noted contributions and concerns demonstrated by this man. Thank you … sir!*

Further, thank you J. Arnold. Ms Arnold is a retired Arkansas educator who was very helpful with my editing process. She proofed, offered incentives, and kept me focused.

To Michael … whom I sometimes refer to as Paul-- I am not sure of your real name; I just remember you as my angel. I am so grateful for your dedication and caring heart. Like me, you did not pre-evacuate nor did you seek sheltered at the Superdome. When the impact of the storm became evident, you sprang into action. That is, you put your life in danger for the sake of saving others. When I descended my roof and boarded your vessel, I was full of praises—thanking God for His blessings and praising you for your courage. Your selflessness will never be forgotten. Since my return to New Orleans, I've searched for you but without success. Nonetheless, if by chance you happen upon this book, or even my first book, In Search of Higher Grounds, *please know that I am forever indebted.*

Further, to my family and friends who, during my period of disconnect, were my eyes, ears, and sounding boards, I appreciate your support and love.

To the citizens of Arkansas who befriended me during my time of need, thank you for giving what you had to offer and accepting what I had to give. Love y'all!

For my readers—critics and advocates, alike—thank you so very much. Without your comments, I view my writing as placid. I appreciate your candor, evaluations, and remarks, without which I would be less inspired to attempt another contribution. It matters not that you agree with my presentation but more that my story has the capability of evoking a response. For the readers who insist that my first installment was far too brief and that they needed additional details in order to achieve closure ... here it is! And for those who perceived my original offering as somewhat shallow or lacking creditability, read on.

Finally, I'd like to thank Charles and Ella Petz of Arkansas. These two people are genuine and caring. They welcomed me into their world and loved me, unconditionally; they offered endless encouragement and support. Moreover, they were extremely instrumental in helping me achieve normalcy during my time of despair. There are no words expressive enough to thank them for their friendship.

Preface

From *In Search of Higher Grounds*, Chapter 32:

I don't know how long I will be in Arkansas, but thus far, I am enjoying life. This is mainly due to my having come to terms with this unconventional yet alluring metropolis. There is still some skepticism, especially when it comes to racial issues; however, I attempt to live each day with an open mind and devoid of controversy. My attempts are not always winning, but more often than not, they are. Having survived Katrina, the convention center, and shelter life, I am no longer easily offended by chauvinist attitudes. After all, if it wasn't for ignorance in the first place, I would not be writing this story. Therefore, it is my belief that God has delivered me to Arkansas for a reason.

Moreover, in recent months as I endeavored to capture my Katrina experience on paper, I have become more enamored of my new home. For in addition to my old friends from New Orleans who are now scattered throughout the United States, I have expanded my network. One can never have too many friends. Still, I miss New Orleans and plan to return one day. When folks question why I would want to go back, they ask if I am not fearful of a reoccurrence. I answer, "Yes, I am afraid, but no one can predict the future, and disasters can happen anywhere, anytime." I suppose a more truthful response would be, "There is nothing like the rapture of your own stomping grounds. The smells, the feel, the quirks and customs are all inbred characteristics of New Orleans that can never be replaced." But until then, each morning I am thankful for God's love, higher grounds, and a new beginning. The spiritual that says, "God is an on time god. He may not come when you call, but he's always on time," is oh so true. During my entire journey, and every time I cried out, God answered. Even when I was in tremendous pain, severe anguish, or unable to recognize His answers, He did not forsake me. Katrina may have been devastating and destructive, but it was also a medium which served God's purpose. I don't pretend to know His plans. I am just content to embrace each day with a joyous spirit and love in my heart. Moreover, I am convinced that most of my journey served to restore my vision and redefine my needs. I know that I am blessed, and I acknowledge that the world is not perfect. Every day I pray for patience and wisdom as I realize, just as Paul advised, "He is not through with me."

INTRODUCTION

Ink Splatters

My official encounter with *Ink Splatters* evolved after the release of my first book, *In Search of Higher Grounds,* published April 2009. Ink Splatters is a collage of ideas and expressions which required release. Writing has always been a form of escape for me. When gloom, despair, or uncertainty overtakes me, I find myself needing to document the cause and effect—I call it chasing ghosts. In the past, I've shared most of my renditions verbally. I've always been capable of embellishing a joke or an already circulating story to the point of reinvention. I suppose in the far corners of my mind, I envision myself to be a more than fair storyteller. However, my quests do not always end with oral presentations. I also enjoy writing. The written word can be quite handy when one is attempting to transfer knowledge, contribute entertainment, or record history. But I find the craft of literary weaving, whether real, fictional, oral, or written, to be challenging, immersing, and thoroughly rewarding. Moreover, I like the idea of being able to bond with my recipients. That's why, with the release of my first book and after I'd received adequate feedback, I knew I wanted to try it again. In addition, since most of the comments received had to do with folks wanting to know, "What happened next?" I thought, "Why not? What a perfect reentry!"

CHAPTER 1

THE ROAD HOME

Although the destruction that occurred along the Gulf Coast during and after Hurricane Katrina in August 2005 is slowly being repaired, there are still many disturbing circumstances that just won't go away. Oh, sure, there is a lot of inspirational growth, construction, and rebuilding along the Coast. However, along with the newness and returning populations, infrastructure and service industries are still lacking. I am Jane Nelson, a native of New Orleans, Louisiana. It took nearly four years after the storm for my home to be completely rebuilt. Moreover, and due to displacement problems, I had to supervise these repairs long distance. This created a lot of unnecessary stress in my life; nonetheless, and as I learned throughout my Katrina journey, God does provide. He delivered me from the storm, and I came to lean on and trust His word. The details of my plight are chronicled in my book, *In Search of Higher Grounds,* written under my pseudonym JoyAnn and published by AuthorHouse. I invited readers to put themselves in my place so that they could share my mindset—in other words, join me as I straddled the catbird seat to ride out the eye of Hurricane Katrina and its aftermath.

Last August, 2010, marked the fifth anniversary of Hurricane Katrina. All along the Coast, people gathered to celebrate and share their stories of perseverance. Moreover, celebrations and political events were staged to show the world that our communities had gotten past the survival stage—that we were no longer victims, but rather healthy, striving metropolitans. However, life sometimes continues to be a struggle. Certainly, metro areas are growing— citizens returning and businesses blossoming. But we are still hindered—overwhelmingly plagued by high unemployment, disturbing crime rates, slow economy, and increased financial burdens. Since publishing my book, I retired from my job at the post office and have returned to my home in New Orleans.

"*So what's next?*" I sometimes ponder. I am home—full time— attempting to establish a comfortable standard of living. My desires are for a peaceful, purposeful existence. Perhaps the answer to my quandaries can be found in my next quest—release of another book. Thus, in addition to labeling myself as survivor, retired reservist, retired civil servant, doting aunt, adoring sister, dependable friend, responsible citizen, proud homeowner, and Child of God, I can now add to my list of characters that of published author.

To be able to capture my ideas on paper in a format enticing to others has always been a priority on my list of goals. In my lifetime, I've written numerous short stories and countless letters as well as other documents. Admittedly, my ability to be lengthy in deliverance is not very good. My thoughts may be acute and engaging, but my presentations are somewhat brief. I am the kind of writer who likes to address the meat of issues without undue hesitation. Which is why, probably, I can compose and tell interesting narratives in a short time. Quite frankly, I might admit that I am an anxious composer. However, I'll take it one step further—I am an equally anxious reader. Therefore, when I am writing a story and reading it at the same time, I often find myself competing in a literary race. I want fulfillment, yet I want it quickly and I want it to be good. Even so, I very much enjoy creative writing. I live for the challenge of being caught up, entangled, or immersed in the art of storytelling. However, my reasons for composing and publishing my first book, *Higher Grounds*, were more out of necessity than for the art of entertainment. You see, prior to Hurricane Katrina, I'd undergone a hip replacement. At the onset of the storm, I was still recovering. Moreover, I was supposedly being prepped for a second surgery. Both hips were affected by A-vascular necrosis. This is a medical term which means that the natural fluids surrounding the joints have dissipated, leaving a dry union. This dryness causes bone-on-bone agitation, which in turn impedes range of motion and causes chronic joint pain.

After the storm and once I had been taken from New Orleans, I was flown to Arkansas; there, I struggled to regain self-reliance. In addition, I sought medical relief. I knew my second procedure could not be put off. I'd foolishly put off the first surgery for eight years. Yes, that's right—eight years! When I was diagnosed and given the prognosis, I would not accept my doctor's proposal. For eight years, I was in denial, determined to heal myself without having to succumb to surgery. I tried exercises, herbs, chiropractor visits, and prayers. But, as my doctor advised, the time came when I finally had to give in to reality. But by the time I conceded to having the procedure, I'd lost a vast percentage of my mobility. I was in so much pain, heavily dependent upon others, and totally humiliated. God humbled me so that I could do nothing more than accept the hand I'd been dealt. After the surgery, I was overjoyed to regain mobility; I was shamed by my stubbornness, yet humbled by God's goodness, for He did not abandon me. I made a solemn vow that I would not go through that nonsense again. Therefore, even though I had no desire for a second surgery, I did not intend to object nor prolong the inevitable.

When I arrived in Arkansas, I did not lose focus. Moreover, even if I had attempted to forget, Arkansas' hilly terrain served as a daily reminder. You see, I, being from New Orleans in what is analytically described as "soup bowl" landscaping, was finding it very difficult to navigate the pathways and streets of Arkansas. Thus once I'd settled in and was able to procure medical help, I made arrangements to undergo the required second surgery. After the surgery and as a form of rehab, I decided that I needed distraction. The distraction came about in the form of composing, releasing, and marketing my book. So in essence, Arkansas gave me the opportunity to complete an item on my bucket list.

I remained in Arkansas a total of four and a half years, from September 2005 to February 2010. In November of 2009, I retired from the post office, and I made my return to New Orleans during February of 2010.

Chapter 2

Decision to Retire

Retirement, although inevitably wasn't an easy choice for me. My assignment to the Little Rock Mail Plant was a blessing. I wanted to reclaim my independency and equally anxious to upright my crumbled world. Please understand, my job, home, finances, and peace of mind were all intertwined. When I arrived in Arkansas in September 2005, I was placed at a youth camp set up as shelter for hurricane victims. Once settled there, I notified my employers of my whereabouts. Prior to the storm, I'd been employed with the post office for nearly fifteen years. At the shelter, I'd learned from news reports that United States President George W. Bush had authorized thirty days of administrative leave for all federal employees who lived along the Gulf Coast and were affected by Hurricane Katrina. While at the shelter I managed to call my employers. I spoke with personnel there and was told that the thirty days administrative leave authorized by President Bush would not apply to postal workers. I was further informed that postal employees would be given ten days of administrative pay but were expected to report immediately for duty at the nearest facility in whichever city or town was closest to them.

These instructions sounded harsh and at the very least impossible to follow. I attempted to explain my position but was cut off with a repeated firm warning: *"Employees who exhaust the ten days grace period will be subjected to leave without pay and may find themselves charged as absent without leave, or at the very most, suspended."* I choked back tears. I knew no amount of explanation would soften these managerial orders. Nonetheless, I knew I had to table these instructions. I had bigger fish to fry. I had to stay focused—remember who was truly at the helm.

You may recall that in my first book, I reported staying at the shelter for roughly six weeks. At the end of that time and due to the small number of participants remaining, the site opted to close. To be fair, that decision was probably best for all. There was so much tension and disrespect on those grounds; it became imperative to end the arrangements. And it wasn't just camp personnel; the turmoil existed on both sides of the color barrier. As reported in my original journal, when some of us evacuees realized that the camp personnel were attempting to "condition" us, we joked about, laughed at, and imitated their mannerisms. However, there were also some in our party who reacted more volatilely at what they perceived to be a conspiracy. They were outwardly threatening toward camp officials. They ranted feverishly at anyone whom they considered to be engaging in discriminatory practices. Their language, tone, and behavior were uncivil. In addition to being offensive, these rebels went out of their way to break camp policies. In actuality, although we did not initiate the fracas, we were nonetheless part of the fray; the entire situation became an embarrassment. Although I considered the staffers to be somewhat judgmental in many of their actions, by the same token, we were at least being given a clean facility, bedding, hot showers, and nourishment. For this I was grateful. No doubt, their condescending attitudes were not warranted, but likewise the militant attitudes demonstrated by some of our self-declared defenders were also unnecessary.

Therefore, the tension at the shelter became intolerable. Many of the evacuees who had families or connections elsewhere chose to leave. I was envious of these folks. Most of my life, I'd been very much without desire to impose or become a burden. And although these circumstances were out of the ordinary, I still could not bring myself to tax my network for accommodations. I stood firm in my convictions. With the rapid exodus of so many evacuees, the camp was eager to end their obligations. The director informed us that it was not cost efficient to continue housing us. In other words, their operational expense far outweighed any government supplement being offered to house hurricane victims. However, the director and his staff agreed to find us accommodations at nearby hotels.

Unfortunately, their idea of nearby hotels did not match mine. The very next morning, we were informed that reservations and transportation had been acquired. We were further instructed that vans would arrive at the camp at 1:00 p.m.; they wanted us packed and ready to travel. Moreover, the hotel was located in Little Rock, Arkansas. At this point, there were only about twelve of us remaining. No one said a word. After a few struggling moments, I spoke up. "Why Little Rock?" I asked.

The director looked in my direction. "What's wrong with Little Rock?" he inquired.

I said, "Nothing, I guess; I just don't know anyone there …"

He cut me off, "And you don't know anyone here." I began to babble, telling him about the apartment I'd arranged to get. I attempted to explain how I was waiting on furniture and that an insurance settlement for my damaged car was scheduled to arrive to this area. I tried to be assertive without sounding irrational. The director threw up his hands; he turned his back and headed out the door. I couldn't hear everything he said but the gist of it was obvious; he was no longer interested.

The other evacuees seemed less concerned about our accommodations. Some even tried to persuade me not to worry, telling me that everything would work out. Although I'd been given more lemons, I wasn't ready to make lemonade. Everyone departed the common area. They were headed toward their assigned barracks to pack. I sat there thinking, attempting to resolve these unexpected turn of events. It was then I noticed one of the female counselors; she had not left the area. She was eyeballing me suspiciously; next, she came over and questioned me. I suppose she was trying to confirm my dilemma. I repeated my predicament. She assured me that she would consult with the director and see if we could get things worked out. When she left, I felt better—not confident, but at least better. I went to my room to pack—just in case. As I half-heartedly began gathering my belongings, I came across my cell phone. I dialed Eloise Peters' number. Eloise is the lady mentioned in my first book; she is white and was a volunteer at the camp. She lived in the community and had been helping me resolve my issues. When she answered, I told her all that had transpired.

Eloise was fierce. "You don't have to go to Little Rock" she said.

"I sure hope not." I answered.

"What time are they coming for you?" she asked. I relayed the answer. Eloise instructed me to inform the director that she would come get me. "I can't get there by one," she apologized. "But I'll be there as soon as possible. Do you want me to call up there and speak to him myself?" she asked. I explained that I'd spoken with a counselor and that she had implied that she'd consult with the director on my behalf, so there might be a possibility that I would not be travelling to Little Rock. Eloise assured me again that I would not have to worry about that. She added, "In fact, you can stay at my house. We've come too far, Jane—getting your furniture, your apartment and other stuff together. Call me after

11

you talk with that lady. I'll know for sure by then what time, if you still need me, I can come pick you up."

Eloise is one feisty lady. I was indeed blessed to have her in my corner. I hadn't called to gain her protection or intervention. I just needed her to echo what I already knew. I wasn't being stubborn. I wasn't attempting defiance; I just needed reinforcement of my ideas. I knew the camp could not force me into Little Rock, yet I had no idea of how I was going to stay on track—remain focused on the business already at hand—reestablishing independence. But God is good! The counselor returned as promised and reported that my accommodations had been changed. Reservations had been made at a local hotel. I departed the shelter that very evening and checked into the hotel; I lived there for two weeks. However, and in reasonable time, I managed to check out of the hotel, move into an apartment, purchase transportation, and reengage a work routine.

Unfortunately, once again misfortune brewed. Late October 2005, I started working at the North Little Rock Postal Plant. Undoubtedly some of you may be asking why the Little Rock office? Short and sweet, I attempted employment at several of the smaller facilities in nearby communities. However, I was given a multitude of excuses ranging from "no position available," or "your physical impairment would be a hazard on the workroom floor," to "the manager was unavailable for interview." I found myself getting further and further away from my goal. So suffice it to say, I just surrendered to ignorance. Rather than get in a big brouhaha concerning equal employment opportunities, I chose to accept a position at the North Little Rock Plant. Nonetheless, there was still quite a bit of mistrust—and thereby tension—resulting from my being hired as a transferee from another office. Primarily, and let me be brief, although the post office, in general, is a federal workplace, it also has its own set of criteria. And the one which directly affected me was being hired into a work place without undergoing the "off-record rite of passage," defined as the challenge of protocol. In essence, the Katrina catastrophe presented me entry into the workforce without penalty or hindrance. I did not have to give up my seniority nor accept temporary placement in order to be employed. Moreover, I was given a clerical position comparable to the one I'd held at the New Orleans Office. This, ladies and gentlemen, goes against the ethical grain of inner-postal procedures. Some managers as well as co-personnel were visibly agitated by my placement. Nonetheless, I was there and other than personal grievances, there was no legal recourse. For weeks, I endured crude whispers, short tempers, dubious questions, and careful monitoring. Nonetheless, I was unmoved by the icy reception; I was there to work and not necessarily to win friends. But God in His infinite wisdom again sent me a bevy of angels. These were the precious few, coworkers and managers alike, who saw beyond my assignment and viewed me with compassion. Whenever they perceived that I was being shut out, they'd stop and share conversations, nothing specific, but blessings nonetheless. I was so very grateful for these Samaritans. I knew I was a good worker and had no need to deviate from the norm, but when you're running from a disaster and find yourself stuck in controversy, it can be frustrating. As time progressed, tempers cooled, questions and monitoring ceased. Although some resentment lingered, it was generally perceived that I was not trying to steal anyone's job nor be disruptive in the workplace. I needed my job and was merely following directives.

As weeks turned into months and my life became less intense, my prayers were of thanksgiving. I asked for God's continued intervention. I'd had enough uncertainties; I needed His help to upright my world. As I'd explained to some of my friends, although my living situation had improved, mentally, I was still trapped inside the proverbial suitcase. Ironically, about this time, the New Orleans Post Office decided to add more fuel to the smoldering chaos. They sent out notice to all of its displaced employees. We were notified that if we intended to keep the positions we'd held prior to the storm, we must return immediately to our home office. Again, I was stunned. I'd been in Arkansas less than six months. The first two months were spent either in the shelter and/or looking for lodgings. I'd been working at the North Little Rock Plant for nearly four months; I was just beginning to get my bearings. And now New Orleans was demanding that all employees who wanted to keep their home station jobs come home—posthaste? Where were we supposed to live? Our homes weren't repaired. And how were we to get home? Where was the extra money coming from to move our newly acquired locks, stocks, and barrels? Moreover, who? Who was going to help us? Why? With all of the suffering we'd endured, why were these administrators rocking our world—again? There weren't any explanations offered, but we were given ten days to comply.

Once again I had been blind-sided. A decision had to be made—and quickly! I wasn't about to place myself in needless peril with stability so close at hand. Thus, based on all the unanswered questions and anticipated fears, I elected to remain in Arkansas; however, ultimately, my decision would be the defining factor used to push me into retirement.

I was basing my actions and decision making on the anticipated repairs to my New Orleans property. It took nearly four years for the construction on my home to be completed. Two of those years were spent in meditation, one year was devoted toward the physical labor, and the last year was spent keeping up appearances. In essence, due to me not knowing beforehand how long I'd be in Arkansas, I'd asked the contractors to work at a leisurely pace. In addition, once the work was done, I still had no idea of when I would be returning. Therefore, after the repairs were finished, the property remained vacant. That worried me, considerably, because I'd become preoccupied with reported break-ins and other criminal activities that were ongoing in New Orleans. I had to pray without ceasing for an answer. God, who does not slumber, heard my pleas. His blessings came about in the form of my contractor finding odds and ends jobs so that they could continue working on my house. It meant extra costs, but it was worth it. The additional labor gave the appearance of activity and I'd hope it would serve as a deterrent against thugs. However, when the major repairs had been completed, I did not rest on laurels; I began requesting transfers back to the New Orleans office. The transfers were denied. Managers and union officials stood in agreement concerning the denial of my requests. They cited my previous election not to return and the nationwide downsizing of postal personnel rosters as bona fide reasons for turning down my transfers. It was at this point that I began to do some serious contemplation; I knew my original plans (pre Katrina) had been to retire in January 2012. I concluded that, although it was nearing November 2009, if the post office was truly downsizing, then it might behoove me to consider an early retirement. My house was finished; I didn't owe any large debt. So I asked myself, "Why not?" Then, as if to put icing on the cake, the post office upped the ante; they offered incentive bonuses for employees opting to retire. I could use the extra cash toward moving expenses. I took these as omens that God was showing me the way out. Although it was a little more than two years prior to my planned retirement, I accepted the early out. It was further mandated by postal directives that personnel who were fifty-five and over (in age) would not be penalized for early retirement. I was nearing sixty. So there was nothing more to contemplate. I was headed home.

CHAPTER 3

HOMECOMING

I returned to New Orleans in February 2010. However, now that I was home, I was filled with other questions, concerns, and agendas. Some of the quandaries were self-imposed while others emanated from family members and friends. Folks asked if and when I would release another book. My answer varied, depending on my mood. Some days, I was hopeful and full of ideas while other days I was brooding and dreading publishing another manuscript. Why? Well, the answer to that deserves its own script—i.e., another book.

As you may recall from my first book, August 29, 2005, is a date forever engraved in my mind. So many things occurring so fast and all at once that it was difficult to digest, yet alone capture and recall. Nonetheless, I did not surrender to Hurricane Katrina nor did I bow to the impact of its proceedings. In addition, I consider myself exceedingly blessed to have been able to release a book describing my journey. Ironically, my trek never really ends; I just found convenient closure points and capitalized upon them. After all, even the best of professionals know when to stop, pause, and gain prospective. Some may summarize this as, "Life is short; stop and smell the roses." However, although I agree that life is short, sometimes the intake is overwhelming. Thus was the case with Katrina; ergo my first book.

As I commence this second attempt at publication, it is mid-2010; I am back in New Orleans, living in my repaired home. August 2010 marks the fifth anniversary of Hurricane Katrina. Although many are still struggling to upright themselves, the immediate focus is on the British Petroleum Oil Spill. Yes, that's right. As the adage implies, "When it rains, it pours." One of my good friends who proclaim herself an Evangelist has captured the very essence of our plight: "kneeling so that we might stand."

These days, along with the ongoing efforts to reunite families, repair property, restore infrastructure, and return to law and order status, citizens of the Gulf Coast are in continuous need of God's blessings. We pray a lot!

If you read my first book, you know that prayer is not a new topic with me. Prior to Katrina, I had some trouble comprehending the need for prayer. But having gone from my rooftop to the hilltops of Arkansas, I learned quickly not only to grasp the necessity of prayer, but also to depend heavily on the answers it supplied.

I have lived in New Orleans all of my life. The fifty-four months I spent in Arkansas is the longest period I've ever lived anywhere other than my hometown. My house and property were completely engulfed by the stagnate waters released by the levee failure during Hurricane Katrina. Just about everything occurring in those five years has been jumbled in my mind. I try very hard, daily, to concentrate and separate the positive aspects of life— variables that demand my immediate attention. Still, I am grateful to be back in my home; I am eager to regain control of my life and am slowly adjusting to the newness and eeriness of everything else. This is a period when old things have become new. In addition to acclimating myself to blighted properties, missing businesses, fewer friends, and lack of community infrastructure, I also have to adjust to new political leaders. New Orleans Mayor Ray Nagin has been replaced by Mitch Landrieu; former Louisiana Governor Kathleen Blanco lost her bid for re-election and Bobby Jindal is now officiating; and George W. Bush, forty third president of the United States, is no longer presiding; in his place is Barrack Obama.

As I maneuver through fog-filled days, I am aware of the many unanswered questions from those who have followed my journey so far. I am not talking about the daily living-type inquiries, but more the big picture inquiries, such as, "How was Arkansas? Do you miss it? Are you still struggling with religious beliefs? How is your health—any hip related maladies? What are you going to do next? Do you like retirement? Are you glad to be home, liking your new house? How is your book faring? Are you planning to write another one?" Moreover, I am also inundated with inquiries from folks who need answers or directions related to their own efforts to become published authors.

So the other day while dividing my time between playing computer games, watching TV, and rummaging for ideas for another book, I asked myself, *Why not kill a flock with one stone?* In other words, why not address all these questions in the format of a second book?

CHAPTER 4:

DO YOU MISS ARKANSAS?

After Katrina, I was flown to Arkansas with many other refugees from the storm. I lived there four and a half years. I made many friends and came to appreciate my new existence; I loved the quiet communities, the family-oriented activities, and the cleanliness of the thoroughfares.

The only drawback to life in Arkansas was the underlying racism. In all fairness, I am not painting the entire state of Arkansas with one broad brush of bigotry, for if not for the genuine folks who befriended and eventually aided me, perhaps my recovery process would not be as successful. When it came time for me to return to New Orleans, I was literally torn. I could not consider turning my back on my hometown, but at the same time, I did not want to leave my new friends nor give up my re-found comfort. I suppose the main reason, other than property ownership in New Orleans that helped me choose in this matter was the low-key bigotry in Arkansas. Although I have much love for those kindred souls who truly opened their hearts and homes to me, I am equally weary and appalled by some of the ignorance and negative practices that also exist there. Having grown up in the South and having lived through civil unrest, I know when I am being disrespected, mocked, or treated unfairly.

When I was a child, there was no recourse—at least none that would make much difference. But as I and much of America matured, most racial disparity dissipated or somewhat lessened. That is, it didn't disappear altogether, but it diminished enough so that the behavior is more or less clandestine or, when it is acted upon, it is met with public criticism. But this cloak-and-dagger racism is alive and brazenly carried out in Arkansas. Many people may disagree with my assessment; however, most of these opponents are white. They will argue that my contentions are either unproven or untrue. However, they are not privileged to both sides of the spectrum; therefore, they cannot, in my opinion, make an effective rebuttal. In the area where I lived, there were very few blacks. I later learned that my apartment(s) were centrally located and that most blacks lived on the other side of town. The majority of my interaction with minorities was at my workplace, Little Rock Post Office, and although the mail plant was a federal facility, it too, catered to some racist posturing. The division there wasn't as prevalent as that found in the surrounding communities, yet, undoubtedly it existed. Still, I was grateful for the transition— being able to regain my independence from shelter life. The subtle racism, physical impairment, and communal living I experienced in the shelter wreaked havoc upon my world. So when I finally transferred to apartment living, I was, like, *Yeah Lord; thank you for Arkansas.* I was especially indebted to the surrounding angels who came to my aid and made my move and transfer easier. Moreover, and most abundantly, I was thankful that God allowed me the ability to discern and persevere.

As I mentioned in my first journal, I am no blush on the rose. In other words, I didn't just fall off the turnip truck. I've worn through many leather soles. Although I was hugely indebted, I knew that Arkansas would not be my final resting grounds. I endured folks making ethnic remarks which I considered borderline slurs; I repeated my sentences for those who professed they couldn't understand my dialect; I made myself visible to those who believed that I should speak only when directly addressed. In other words, I did my best to be me without being aggressive.

I did not hide nor back down from confrontations; instead, I met them straight on. I was neither belligerent nor demanding. I allowed folks to know that I was human and expected to be treated as such. My contentions received many good responses as well as some rejections. There were those who tried to persuade, correct, or convince me of error judgment while others ignored me entirely. Nonetheless, I am grateful to those who accepted me without perverse stipulation. *Yea, Lord ... I put on Your whole suit of armor.* I managed to give some leeway to my oppressors without compromising my self-esteem.

For example, when I moved into my first apartment, I felt liberated. Living at the camp was not ideal for me. While there, I had to surrender not only to administrative policies but to communal rituals as well. The camp very much reminded me of my brief encounters on the streets of New Orleans during the aftermath of Hurricane Katrina or the ruckus which ensued at the convention center as we waited rescue. As you may recall, in my original story I told of the unpleasantness and sub-human conditions I experienced in those arenas. Well, shelter life, although more contained, still flushed out the need of some to be self-serving. I don't know what it is about disasters that can bring about the worst in mankind. Again, I am not broad-brushing humanity, because there were many caring souls who went out of their way to be generous and giving. But for the most part, I quickly learned that in order to survive, I needed to keep my senses sharpened. Nonetheless, when you are being publicly housed, you really don't have much sway powers. Thus when I found an apartment and was able to move in, I welcomed the return of my privacy. I wasn't looking at this move as a black or white issue, but merely as self-preservation. Unfortunately, not long after I settled into the community, the matter of bias once again began to present itself.

My rent was supposedly being paid by FEMA (Federal Emergency Management Agency). This was *lagniappe* and truly a blessing! However, FEMA bureaucracies started giving everybody the blues. Their on-and-off-again warnings about ceasing rent payments created uncertainty and subsequent mistrust. As such, the manager of my apartment suggested that I pay my own rent. I was somewhat embarrassed. However, I understood her point. After all, I was employed; FEMA was putting out mixed signals—so without argument, I complied. The next month, I received a telephone call from FEMA. They were asking me to send documents to help them process and continue my rent assistance. I declined, telling them that since they stopped paying my rent, I had no difficulties doing it on my own. The clerk informed me that my rent payments had not stopped. I told her that my leasing manger and I had each gotten written notices and numerous phone calls telling us that the rental program was ending. The woman apologized for the misunderstanding; she assured me that the program was still operational. She further told me that, according to their records, my payments were still being made. *WHAT?!*

I informed them that I'd paid my rent last month and was

scheduled to make another payment at the end of the current week. The clerk recommended that I speak with my apartment manager, because a check on my behalf had gone out last month and another check for the current month had also been issued. I was in complete shock. What exactly was going on? I told the FEMA clerk that I would call their office after I'd resolved the rent payments with my complex manager.

That very evening I spoke with personnel at my leasing office. I told them what had transpired and asked them to please explain. I could see by their exaggerated expressions that they were not in the mood. But I was persistent. Finally, the rental manager agreed to speak with me. She informed me that she'd checked the records and, yes, there had been a double payment made on my apartment last month. She further stated that due to FEMA warnings, it might be a good idea to allow this error to go uncorrected. This way when FEMA did officially stop making payments, I'd have a credit balance on my account. *WHAT?*

I politely refused the offer. I informed her that when and if FEMA ended the program, I would be more than happy to produce any money I owed to my creditors. Again, she gave me an exaggerated look. She pursed her lips, shrugged, and then replied, "Well, let me get with my supervisor, and then I'll get back to you." Three weeks later and after numerous attempts to get my money, I filed a small claims case against her. When she was served the court documents, my money was immediately returned. We did not have to go to court.

However, as an offset, my car was subsequently vandalized. My mama didn't raise no fool ... I knew to continue in this arena would be futile, so I moved on. God blessed me with another apartment and with the help of caring souls, I managed the necessary transfer. Moreover, due to FEMA inconsistencies concerning rent aid, I opted to decline any further rental assistance. I didn't like the feeling of being compromised, I didn't care for all the red tape, and I felt the temptation of greed might be too much for any unscrupulous landlords.

Once I'd settled into my new digs, I arranged to undergo my very needed and pending surgery. After the procedure, I commenced a walking routine. Early one morning while strolling along the drive way of the new complex, I was nearly run over. It was about 4:00 a.m.; I chose that time of day because of the absence of traffic. I was enjoying a comfortable pace when I sensed a car trailing me. I ignored it; I figured the driveway was wide enough for two cars to pass without incident, so if the driver was attempting to get around me, it should not be a problem. Moreover, there were no other vehicles on the road. At first the car was moving very slowly but as it neared, the speed increased. I turned around and was suddenly frozen on the spot. The headlights barreled toward me; I didn't know what to do. I called out, but the car kept coming forward. Scanning quickly my entire perimeter, I saw a fire hydrant to my right. It was positioned on top of a cement slab. It was only a couple of feet away, so I feverishly jumped in that direction. The driver swerved his wheels, barely missing me, the hydrant, and the curb. I stood there staring as the car continued to move onward without further incident. I screamed wildly and immediately scavenged my surroundings, looking for a rock or stick in case this idiot planned to return. I did not find a weapon but thanked God that the callous creep did not return. Once I'd settled down, I began to process what had transpired. I concluded my walking that early in the morning had somehow stirred up ignorance. I further rationalized that I, too, was partially to blame. I did not use common sense or due diligence. Here it was four o'clock in the morning and I was walking, alone. It was a predominantly white section of town and when the car approached, I did not give credence to possible harm. I should not have put so much trust in the fact that the apartment was gated. I obviously had insulted the driver by not acknowledging his car or his space; in retrospect, my absentmindedness and seemingly dismissive attitude probably escalated the driver's desire to teach me a lesson. I really needed to be more alert and less assuming.

Another example of me being unaware has to do with the exchange of common courtesy. I'd scheduled an appointment with a local podiatrist; I arrived at his office early. As I entered the waiting area, I saw the receptionist. She was white and was seated in a small cubicle. The bottom section of her area was a half desk with protruding counter space. The top space was represented by a glass window. The window could slide opened or closed, allowing the receptionist some privacy. In the waiting area were two ladies, also white. One of them appeared slightly older while the other could easily have been my age. The two women sat next to each other, leading me to presume they were together. The waiting area was nothing more than a large room furnished with chairs, television, coffee tables, and a large supply of popular but dated magazines. As I entered, my very hearty and sincere salutation, "Good morning," was met with complete silence. I was livid but mostly embarrassed. *Ah, my first snub of the day,* I mentally analyzed.

Nonetheless, I took a seat. Just before reaching for a magazine, I said aloud, "Good morning, Lord, for I know you hear me," and I began thumbing through the magazine. Again, silence. A few awkward seconds later, the receptionist looked up and motioned me to her area. I walked over, answered a few questions, and in general, confirmed my appointment. I returned to my chair. The room was eerily quiet; again I picked up the magazine. I thumbed it quickly, not really reading. I quietly asked God to give me restraint. I had to keep reminding myself that everyone was not receptive to good manners. I had to stop trying to convert folks. Moreover, I had to stop being so grossly affected by rejection. The receptionist closed her window. That left us three patients in a heavily strained environment. Nevertheless, we sat there, each pretending that all was well. Not so soon afterward, I heard this small, soprano voice infiltrate the dead air. "My, that's a pretty outfit you have on." It was the younger woman who spoke. The senior smiled and nodded in my direction. Well, I didn't know how to respond—these were my same clothes; I had not changed.

However, I didn't want to be overtly snotty, for I recognize an olive branch when one is being offered. Still, on the other hand, I was upset about the amount of time it took for these ladies to recognize and become civil toward me. Nonetheless, I politely thanked them for their compliment and continued rifling the magazine. I knew that the two were trying to make amends but my perception of the matter had already been formulated. The whole thing was unnecessary foolishness. Fortunately for us all, the receptionist slid the glass window open and announced to the women, "The doctor will see y'all now." I inhaled deeply and exhaled slowly; I allowed my thoughts to drift elsewhere.

One might conclude that Arkansas is indicative of most of America. There is good and evil everywhere. However, what impressed me most about Arkansas is the numerous churches and countless denominations. You'd think from those prospects, religious practices would be second nature to their way of living. And for the most part, it may be. But amongst their citizenry are many who merely cower behind the cross. These are the citizens who are quite adept at dispensing arrogance along with acts of righteousness. They use the cross as a scepter; when caught in the crosshairs, they will be the first to profess Christianity. I believe the incident surrounding my move in and out of my second apartment supports this theory.

I lived in my first apartment ten months (October 2005 to August 2006). I moved into my second apartment in September 2006 and lived there nearly forty months (September 2006 to

February 2010). Prior to moving into this gated community, I'd been told that there would be a two-week waiting period. This was an inconvenience, but not a deal breaker. Upon my move-in day, I arrived and went straight to the leasing office. There I filled in and signed a rental agreement. Copies were made, instructions rendered, and the key provided. Just before I left the office, the clerk said, "Oh, one more thing, Ms. Jane. As you know, your apartment is a handicapped unit. The previous tenant was confined to a wheelchair. He also had some anger management problems. As such, some of the walls, cabinets, and appliances may have dings and dents in them. We've cleaned up a lot, but please go in and inspect the apartment and if you find anything you believe needs additional repair or replacement, let us know."

I sat there staring at her. She waited for my response. I didn't offer one. She next proceeded to lambaste me for lack of gratitude. "Look," she informed me. "I didn't have to tell you anything. I am a Christian and I wanted to do the right thing."

Well, that was enough to loosen my tongue. "No, I believe the right thing would have been for you to tell me prior to my signing these documents. More than likely, I'd still have taken the apartment since I am already here. But if there is previous damage, then clearly if you were exercising righteousness, your disclosure should have been proffered prior to obligating my finances."

If looks could kill, I'd have been scurrying up the King's Highway. Anyway, although she was not forthcoming, I had no other option but to move in. When I moved out in February 2010,

Eloise, I, and several others cleaned that apartment, leaving it immaculate. Would you believe the managers still manufactured excuses that allowed them to keep additional amounts of my security deposit? Before moving out, I'd requested a walk-through, but the manager declined, stating it was not necessary. I was instructed to leave my apartment key in the external lock box, which I did. I was further advised that my security deposit would be forwarded to my new address. However, when the check arrived, it was noticeably short. I did not complain; instead, I accepted their trumped-up reasons and reduced funds. I did, however call and leave the following message: "Thank you very much. I do not agree with your assessment because I left that apartment in better condition than it was received. During my tenure, I kept up with and reported all necessary repairs; further, I did not break anything. However, my God is awesome. So if you're satisfied with your rendering, then, Praise Him!" They did not offer debate; they hemmed and hawed ... then cited some generic language about maintenance and standard fees which were supposedly applicable.

Arkansas was my training field--while there, I learned patience and how to let go and to let God. He is my Redeemer and Way Maker. Although I was confronted sometimes daily by trivial nonsense, I prayed for empowerment. As a result, I resolved to pick my battles wisely. And this worked; admittedly, it was kind of tricky at times, but slowly it became less harrowing. I began to view racial slurs or inferences as more a war of words—of which I had plenty. In addition, other encounters had to do with me vying for attention and/or service as store clerks and other service industry employees pretended they did not see me. As discouraging as this may sound, I persevered. I was determined to keep my promise to stop chasing ghosts. I had a roof over my head, reliable friends, a car, and a job. Essentially, I'd survived the storm; I wasn't about to get turned around by arrogant attitudes—neither on my part or that of others. Having reached that conclusion, and although exceedingly blessed, I knew my journey had not ended—I needed to continue my search for higher grounds. Little did I know my trek would end at the very place in which it began.

I'd observed and learned a lot while in Arkansas. Most of my memories are pleasant; unfortunately, and as with most worldly matters, some are not. By this, I mean some folks were true and caring Christians, but others—not so much.

Much of the unpleasantness directed toward me, I kept secret. In the beginning I tried to share some of the incidents with my new friends, but my stories were dismissed, ignored, or explained as acts of "mean-spirited" individuals. As such, I quickly rationalized my supporting hosts were unwilling to address or act upon such matters. And, actually, I was okay that it played out that way. I did not blame anyone for not wanting to get involved. I figured to do otherwise could intensify racial discord. After all, I was being mocked and shunned, not murdered. There was no need to rock the boat or make mountains out of molehills.

Therefore, my time in Arkansas was perversely burdened. I

was surrounded by many wonderful people, a few tormentors, and some unresolved controversies. Moreover, when my book was published, the discrepancies increased. I believe this occurred mainly because many who were helping me obviously thought that no matter the circumstances I would not jeopardize my standing. However, when they read that I was publicly calling attention to some of the bigotry practiced in Arkansas, some were not pleased. Many of the agitators tried to malign my testimony. They alleged that I was being unappreciative and implied that my book contained inaccuracies and hurtful allegations. As the situation heated up, I was even approached by several who pretended to extend olive branches; they offered fake apologies and expressed crocodile remorse for any unfair treatment perpetrated against me during my stay at the shelter. Their scheme was to weave a false sense of security which might provoke me to recant my story. Their ploy was unsuccessful. I refused to abate my position. I explained that my accounting was my personal experience. Moreover, dealing with racist attitudes was not the most devastating event of my journey. I reminded them of the intensity of the storm; I emphasized the discomfort of communal living. I rationalized the necessity of managing groups of people; I threw in cultural differences. But my answers fell upon deaf ears. These folks weren't looking for explanations. In retrospect, I believe these instigators had already condemned me and were merely camouflaging their pre-planned attack. The penalty I incurred was in being excluded from social circles. Of course, this did not include everyone. However, although the division was more prevalent in the communities, it also carried over into my workplace.

At the Little Rock post office, only a few mangers seemed to dislike my book. Their response was to skirt discussing the book with me; however, since they continued to treat me fairly, I was okay with their response. In addition, by the time the book came out, the New Orleans office was up and running. I was fortunate to be able to negotiate sales to both facilities. As far as I know, and even though I got some tongue in cheek responses, none of my co-workers from either facility expressed being offended by my journal. Although my book stirred up and created communal debates, my major battle was to diffuse some of the resentment being expressed by the local citizenry of Arkansas. It was an uphill battle, but it wasn't all one sided. Those who accepted my presentation expressed their delight, while those who felt I was being unfair or that I was undermining their "good works" were determined to make me an outcast.

Thank God, their planned attack, although hurtful, did not create further anguish. Moreover, in the interim, I learned that the shelter where I'd been housed when I arrived in Arkansas, the one I had referenced in my book, was affiliated and deeply rooted in the communities. I supposed I could have made this discovery prior to publication, but my story wasn't about affiliation. Nor was it about organizations. I was mostly interested in relaying my journey from my mindset; I wanted my readers to be inside my head and to decipher matters as I encountered them. Nonetheless,

I felt the townspeople's pain and understood why they wanted to discredit me. However, I refused to give in to their accusations. I allowed them to know that, for the most part, I was truly grateful for all that Arkansas provided. Still, it did not erase the ugliness that also existed. Although I was unmoved, I was no bumpkin. I allowed them to react and respond without significant response from me. In the end, those who were genuine continued their embrace and those who were not demonstrated their anger by withdrawing social pleasantries. Nonetheless, the whole ordeal was revelation. God is good! With the release of my book, a lot of people realized that I was a lot more observant than I let on. I got the feeling that either they thought I had been oblivious to some of the equal-but-separate practices or that I was so comfortable with the manner in which I was being treated that I would not risk calling unfavorable attention to my benefactors. But avoidance is not me; I believe fair is fair.

Moreover, and I am the first to admit that I am only human and therefore subject to error, I pride myself on attempting to be respectful of others. I treat folks in the manner that I desire to be treated. As comfortable as Arkansas had become and as desperately as I needed their help, I could not continue to silently accept neither subtle nor random acts of supremacist behavior. Therefore, as the disgruntling acts continued and tensions became undeniable, I knew it was time to move on. This was sad; nonetheless, it was necessary. Ironically, God's plans became abundantly clear—the demonstrated withdrawal by some community members, the forced retirement from the post office, along with the completion of my home were almost simultaneous. Still, I do not take back my proclamation: Arkansas provided me temporary solace. It was my rock in the storm and therefore, it was my higher grounds. Coming from the convention center in New Orleans, having to endure shelter and communal living, as well as reestablishing self-reliance, transportation, and a work routine … Arkansas provided for my needs adequately. I was moderately happy and comfortable there. The racism, although scary, was mostly low-key. With the exception of the road rage incident, in hindsight, my survival was inevitable. In conclusion, yes, of course I miss Arkansas. I met people there who saw me at my lowest form and yet embraced me. I met folks there who demonstrated beyond belief the Christian love described in the bible. I have permanent friends there. Their kindness touched me so deeply; I know without doubt that this is all a part of the Master's plan. Very often and especially when I am feeling helpless, I use the memories of Arkansas, in their entirety, to remind me of God's blessings!

CHAPTER 5

AM I STILL STRUGGLING WITH RELIGIOUS BELIEFS?

At the onset of Hurricane Katrina I was riding a wave of apathy. I had come to accept my life as sad and unproductive. Proverbs 22:6 advises that one should "train up a child so that when he or she is old, he or she will not stray from the path." This is sage advice; however, it was wasted on me, for although my upbringing mandated that we attend church, the biblical lessons being taught there did not carry over into our home life. My father, as you may recall, was an immigrant; his ideas concerning religion were restricted to "do as I say ... not as I do" parenting. He wanted us to attend church, but I can never ever recall seeing him there. Most of his time was spent working. And if his activities weren't directly work related, he was involved in social bonding with his sea buddies; my father was a cook aboard a steamship. More specifically, my father was from Panama; he stowed away on a liner that had been docked near his village. The crew kind of adopted him; they taught him English and a trade. They helped him get his American citizenship. My father was a good student when it came to emulating his sea pals. Unfortunately, most of the values he gleaned were superficial. Surely, those sea mates helped him achieve personal goals, but my father was very much unable to grasp the full idea of responsibilities—especially when it came to family values. For these reasons, and although my father insisted that we, his offspring, attend church and go to school, he really had no interest in our development.

Thus, once I decided to pursue life on my own, I felt it unnecessary to continue the tomfoolery of church and inevitably I abandoned school rituals next. In my first book, I confessed to quickly changing my stance concerning education. This world, if nothing else, revolves around educational levels. In the beginning of my independence I was overjoyed. I was able to obtain a decent job doing manual labor in the service industry. I was ecstatic to have my own money and apartment, but more importantly, I did not have to answer to anyone but me. However, not long after proclaiming my independence, my happiness began to wane. Although the money was steady, I discovered that I had very few choices in life. I couldn't afford vacations; I did not know how to drive, could not afford a car; and on top of that, I was scarcely living payday to payday. What I had perceived as freedom at the beginning was actually a stagnate existence. I was miserable.

I lamented, searched for answers, and cried. Why was this happening to me? I'd run away from home because I thought surely I could do better on my own. Although answers eluded me, miraculously, I managed to blame all of my downfalls on God. I believe God became my scapegoat because I realized that I could no longer fault my father's supervision or lack thereof for my failures. I remember thinking, *I'll never be happy; God does not love me. If He did, I would not be going through this mess. When I was little, there was no one there for me, and now that I'm grown ... why am I still abandoned? What is it I'm doing wrong ... what is the criteria for His love?*

After long self-examinations and conversations, I decided I had to go back to school. I decided that in order to better myself, I needed to get better educated. Moreover, I wasn't just thinking short term but long term as well. I wanted to attend college. Next, I began researching ways of accomplishing these tasks that would not drain me financially. In my search, I discovered the military.

I read that Uncle Sam would pay for college tuition in exchange for tours of duty. So now I had a firm plan.

Many years later, I'd achieved most of my goals, I was better educated, was able to attain better jobs, and was well on my way to success. I'd purchased a house and had my own car; I'd even been blessed with travels both within the States and abroad; moreover, I had significant savings, yet there was very little joy in my life. Once again, I had to reexamine my world. I concluded what was missing was Jesus. It seemed it didn't matter how affluent, educated, or well-bred I was, my world was inexplicably empty. This is when I invited Him into my life. Times were hard and I was tired; I needed Him at the helm. And this is where my book, *In Search of Higher Grounds,* picks up and unfurls. I was not totally convinced He existed, but I was willing to take the chance.

By the end of the book, I am enthralled by his love. I am wondering how in the world I made it in this world without truly knowing Christ. Moreover, my stay in Arkansas is exemplary of His love. Admittedly, all things were not perfect … but all things are possible through Him. The angels that rescued and literally took me under their wings were my assurance of His love. I cried many a night, and I wrestled endlessly with my decision making, but in the end, it was He who brought me through. He not only lifted me spiritually, but His love spilled over into my ordinary life. This is probably why I am still missing my Arkansas Sunday morning worship service. When I met Eloise at the shelter, she began to tell me about her church. She was so enthusiastic and bubbly as she described the people, events, and lessons. Her talks and subtle invitations finally won me over. I had to go and share in that spiritual camaraderie. And I did. Those women, whom I later dubbed the Sunday school ladies, were nothing but nice to me. They hugged, kissed, prayed, and won their way into my heart. For the most part, I'm not usually a touchy-feely individual. Upon meeting these new friends, I was kind of standoffish. But these ladies weren't having any of that nonsense. They gave me my space, but their congenial spirit stole its way into my world. It wasn't long before I was charmed by Christianity. I love those women, and their exemplary embrace became contagious; I was finding love and feeling uplifted throughout the sanctuary … and, yes, even in the community. I am not saying arrogance became a thing of the past because arrogance, like evil, will continue to evolve. Nonetheless, there was something about those parishioners that kept me excited about Christ. I found myself eager to share and be a part of their praises. In addition, when I was occupied with Godliness, I was able to set aside much of the worldly differences that sought to bind me. When I worshipped, fellowshipped, and studied with those angels, my world was joyous. The sermons, missions, and shared hymns enlightened and persuaded me that God so loved the world … me included.

Now that I am back in New Orleans, I have once again grown weary. I know that He is alive, and I continue to praise His holy name. It's just that the church home where I am now a member is not very inspiring. Perhaps I should explain that this is the same facility I attended prior to the storm and, as previously stated, at that time, I was merely going through the motions. But now, after deliverance from Katrina and having experienced the awesomeness of the Arkansas sanctuary, I find myself drifting. I am aware that my current church is still very much affected by post-Katrina matters. Our facility is still at this writing in a state of disrepair. But that is not the main culprit. There's dwindling membership, too. Not everyone is back—but those who have returned are not very responsive. I don't know the whole constraints and confines that prevent our church from pursuing God's work, but it is obvious that we are at a laboring crossroad. I am prayerful for unity and renewed spirit. I hold in my heart a departing message whispered to me from one of my Arkansas sisters: "Never give up on God, Jane. He loves you and will never abandon you. He is everywhere."

Nonetheless, I am humbled and pleased that there is love for me in both communities— Arkansas and New Orleans. When I consult with my Christian siblings concerning church affairs, they offer condolences, hope, and prayers. Hallelujah!

CHAPTER 6

HOW IS YOUR HEALTH?

I suppose I am like most folks when it comes to health care—I'd like to fantasize that all is well. Moreover, since I also hate going to doctors, I don't agonize over slight misgivings. However, before the storm, I occasionally went back and forth for routine exams. I mostly went when it became necessary. The times prior to my hip ailment found me ducking and dodging health care with great stealth. However, after undergoing my surgeries, I still manage to neglect primary care. There is no explanation or justification for my antics; I just do not like medical rituals. I concede that some of you may be nodding in understanding while others may be shaking your heads in disbelief. Nevertheless, I make no excuses.

As previously noted, to speed up my healing process, I began a walking routine when I lived in Arkansas. Once I returned to New Orleans, I purchased a treadmill. I did this because for months after my return I did not walk. I wasn't too sure about walking the streets of my hometown. Reported criminal activities, unpaved streets, unlit or broken streetlights, and general pride prevented me from exposing myself to the elements. But after several months without a physical routine, my mobility began to falter. I was having trouble breathing and my gait was weakening. So without further delay, I went out and purchased a treadmill. It wasn't a cheap trekker. I wanted something that was going to inspire and motivate me. I knew if I paid a considerable amount for a reputable brand, I was going to use it. I've always been somewhat of a miser. Nonetheless, taking in account my age and medical history, my health is average; In other words … it is what it is.

Many readers asked about my hips. Where do I begin? As for the physical condition of them, I feel no pain. However, immediately after my return to New Orleans, Johnson and Johnson began a recall of hip implant devices. I believe the brand name of the recalled prosthetics was DePuy. Now, you know I was not ready for that. I found myself once again on my knees. Having had two hip replacements, both of them performed during the time of the issued recalled items—this was heartbreaking. God led me to contact my first orthopedic surgeon. He was still practicing in New Orleans. I made an appointment with him; he took X-rays of both hips and provided me with medical records of the first operation. He assured me that the model he'd implanted was not the recall brand. He further stated the X-rays showed that the implant inserted by the Arkansas surgeon was also not the recall brand.

To say I was relieved would be an understatement. Nonetheless, because I wanted the surgical records from the second procedure, I requested my records from Arkansas. At the beginning of November 2010, I had chance to return to Arkansas for a brief visit. While there I drove to the orthopedist's office to pick up my records. The clerk requested that I sign for the documents, and I did. A few minutes later the records specialist came out. She had a second release statement that required my signature. "I've already signed release forms," I told her.

Nonetheless, she clutched the papers to her chest, smiled sweetly, and informed me, "These are for the doctor." Not wanting to cause a stir and not quite sure why the doctor would want a separate signing, I signed the documents. She handed me the records and I left. I put the papers in my suitcase and went on with the rest of my visit.

Several weeks later while packing for another trip, I opened my suitcase and found the coveted document stored in a zippered compartment. I sat down and began reading the report. I got halfway through and was immediately sick to my stomach. This was supposedly a routine report detailing a medical procedure. However, what I was reading was more like a cover-up. It appeared the replacement did not go as anticipated. From what I read, the surgeon had miscalculated the size of the implant he used for my surgery. The bottom half was attached successfully but when he attempted to join the top, he ran into difficulty. He was going to change the whole unit out but concerns arose about removing the bottom half. Ultimately he resolved the entire matter by joining the ill-fitting top to the already in place bottom with the use of surgical screws.

However, as he was dictating the procedure, he was also ranting about my physical size. It was as though he felt it necessary to distract from his error by calling attention to my girth and possible poor choices in life. "Patient is obese; morbidly huge. There are layers of fat obstructing and making this procedure extremely difficult. Patient admits alcohol intake but denies tobacco or drug abuse ..." I could not read any further. Who was this person? I chose him as my surgeon but, my God, this man was diabolic!

I began thinking about how I came to choose him as my orthopedist. I mentally rehashed the pre-consultations I'd had with him. Moreover, I slowly begin to piece together the warning signs I'd obviously ignored. This surgeon had been recommended by my new friends. I consulted with him prior to my surgery and shared my many concerns—specifically, my weight. He seemed genuinely compassionate. At no point did he express doubt or anxiety. As a matter of fact, he was very calming; he concurred that my weight gain was most likely due to loss of mobility. I'd explained to him my denial, distractions, and dilemma. He was told that for nearly ten years I could not walk without use of support. He asked about drug, alcohol, and tobacco usage but did not admonish or register alarm.

But now, as I sat on my couch clutching this transcript, I began to wonder just how wrong my procedure had gone. This surgeon was obviously trying to cover his mistakes by throwing me under the bus. I remembered immediately after my surgery, there had been an attempt to discharge me from the hospital. I refused the dismissal. I requested the hospital allow me an additional forty-eight hours. I explained that I needed more time to recover. Although it appeared that they did not want to honor my request, they allowed me to stay. I needed to ensure that once I left the hospital, my ability to manage and maneuver independently would be intact. I thought their proposal was a little strange, but I did not pursue the matter. Ironically, my doctor did not visit me during my recovery period. I was seen by one of his assistants. Further, when I went for my postop exam at his office, I was once again seen by an assistant. At that time, I was briefed concerning my surgery. I recall being told that as a precaution during my surgery, the doctor placed two screws to attach my implant to ensure a secured union. That was it! I was instructed that I need not return for future visits unless I started experiencing discomfort or pain. I was further advised that walking would enhance my mobility. Walking? Just walking? No more appointment? No rehab or follow-ups? This was indeed strange because I remembered my first surgery in New Orleans. After that procedure, I was scheduled for rehab and continued post exams until the orthopedist was sure I could manage on my own. My treatment had lasted six months. However, as I admitted, I am not a medical fanatic. This Arkansas person was releasing me. For the most part, my pain was gone; I was still on medical leave from my job. So it was up to me to work things out. And I did—I walked it out.

Although I was disturbed about all the weird theatrics surrounding the hospital and my physician, I was determined not to chase ghosts. I did not view the orthopedists' misgivings as racist; instead, I defined his antics as gluttonous. I surmised that the doctor was not who I believed him to be. I further concluded that his initial display of compassion and assurances were mere Academy performances. He had been listed as an authorized medical provider within my insurance network. Most likely, he knew this procedure would be costly and that he would get paid without hindrance. Thus, his objective was not skin tone but rather the color of money. This angered and disappointed me. Yet I managed to dismiss him from my world just as quickly as he'd dismissed me. That was then. Now, as I sat and read over his report, I realized that there was more evil to this man than I initially suspected. Not only did he botch my surgery, but he had the audacity to try and place me at fault. Granted, my behavior and choices in life may have been contributors to my physical impairment, but his miscalculation no doubt was the lone cause for the debacle taking place in that operating room. And as if to add insult to injury, it suddenly became quite clear why the record specialist would not release my records until I signed a second document. "It's for the doctor," she'd said. And indeed, most likely it was … a release from malpractice pursuit.

Halfway through my rage, I experience calmness. It was as though God had His Hand over my heart, reminding me, "You're no longer in pain; you are able to walk and stand without using support. Why are you discouraged? I am your Doctor, Lawyer, and Healer."

"Yea, Lord; how quickly we forget." So in His name, I proclaim myself to be whole, healthy, and blessed.

CHAPTER 7

<u>Now That You Are Home, What Are Your Plans?</u>

Now what? Now that I am home, a lot of familiarity is missing. I find myself struggling to fit in. It sometimes feels as though I never left Arkansas. But I digress. Today's New Orleans reminds me very much of a dog chasing its tail; we seem to be having fun, but the impact is still overwhelming and dizzying. Everyone, from politicians to street vendors, wants to emphasize that nothing has changed. We are supposedly in the same place; it's as though Katrina never happened. However, nothing could be further from the truth. There is a lot of emptiness in New Orleans. And I am not just talking about missing people, properties, and businesses; I am talking spirit. Folks go out of their way to pretend "N'awlins" is still here. And I suppose that's mostly due to this being a tourist town. But between the partying, street swagger, "second lines," and savory foods, there appears to be a vacancy of emotions. One might almost detect hesitancy ... as though we are all waiting for the other shoe to drop. And who's to say ... perhaps the missing shoe is represented by the recent oil spill in the Gulf.

I love New Orleans; I love the food and I adore my family and friends, but each morning I awake to a gnawing emptiness. I am no longer complacent but that's a good thing—I hope. Moreover, I am no longer self-absorbed. There are so many professionals who no longer practice or own businesses in our communities. Each time I need something accomplished, it is without doubt going to be a treasure hunt to find a service provider. Medical appointments, dental needs, clothes, furniture, appliances, groceries, and other necessities have now become scavenger hunts. You have to scope, scout, and plan what would otherwise be ordinary trips. And may God help you if you're not privy to your own transportation, or at least computer savvy.

I suppose I could spend hours ranting about the economy or

the lack of moral ethics. I don't know which frightens me more. As a Christian, I am appalled by the murderous attitudes which have befallen our future generation. Every day the media broadcasts some demoralizing incident that leaves us all just shaking our heads. You would think that after Katrina, there would be more of a harmonic atmosphere, right? But instead it is quite the opposite. It is my belief that due to the martial law established during and after Katrina, many criminals heightened their momentum and increased their quest for power. My rationalization is that martial law did not discourage those thugs who chose not to evacuate. These hoods instead saw the city as wide open and ripe for criminal gains. With no legal enforcement intact to control their vultures' ways, these lawbreakers felt they were above the law. They installed their own brand of justice. Their reign of terror became rampant. Each one greedily competed for vacant properties and territories. However, now that I am home, I also conclude that these evil predators were not very far advanced in their thinking. They obviously had not considered the return of property owners or the reinstatement of legal pursuits. Moreover, I believe today the criminals are demonstrating their frustration more so through use of insane acts of brutality. They feel threatened, so in order to continue sovereignty, they are attempting to recreate mass hysteria. However, I serve a God who sits high and looks low. The citizens, government, and police are slowly shifting the balance of power. It's not easy, and we realize it will not take place overnight. Nonetheless, we must persevere. Now that legal forces and properties are being recovered, the criminals must be relegated to the rocks from which they crawled. Am I scared? Of course—but I know that Jesus is alive, and I refuse to live my life in bondage. He will not abandon us.

Second on my list of concerns is the escalating economy. Being on a fixed income is quite edgy. I try not to get bogged down by rising finances or lack thereof. I try to live one day at a time, which means I often find myself having to recalculate my living expenses each month. Everything has gone up—home insurance, sanitation fees, utilities, cable, telephones—just to name a few. I often think about whether I will have to get a job to supplement my retirement income. I have no qualms about having to return to the labor market, but if I had my druthers, I would prefer not to. I have labored nearly forty-five years; I have not once turned to stealing or any other illegal activities to support my needs. Now that I have reached my twilight years, I so much want it to be leisure living. I am not talking an extravagant lifestyle, just one that is pleasantly sufficient. In essence, I want to make and live according to my own itinerary. Mayhap you can conclude my thinking in this matter is very much along the lines of the Israelites. They too labored for forty years before being allowed to enter the Promised Land. Nonetheless, my thoughts in these matters are not etched in stone. If He so dictates, I will follow. Nonetheless, I am not ashamed to admit my current desires are lean toward abstinence from labor.

Friends and family members continue to plague me with inquiries concerning my future. I usually just shrug and blow off their questions. I don't know how to explain this fog that envelopes me. So far, the only thing which seems to pique my interest is authoring another book. However, although I have the interest, I am stumped for a subject matter. I wrote my first book because I felt a need for distraction. I needed to unload. So much had transpired and so much had transformed, I needed to heal and recoup. Thus, *In Search of Higher Grounds* was penned. But now that I am home, officially retired, and with much time of my hands, I find myself without specific subject matter.

Certainly, there is no reason to continue blowing up Katrina, and there is no need to filter through the British Petroleum Oil Spill of April 2010. The only thing left is to describe the underlying bleakness which hovers over New Orleans. And actually, I don't want go there, again. I am going to take the advice of our recently elected mayor, Mitch Landrieu, I am going to quit living in the past. In one of his platform speeches, Mayor Landrieu urged citizens to quit talking about New Orleans in the past tense. He further admonished that we are past that survival stage and are living in the phoenix stage of rebirth—not struggling. However, I am not sure he is completely right. New Orleans has come a long way, but things are not all good. The crime rate continues to grow. Unemployment levels are dangerously high. Taxes, levees, mileages are steadily eroding our nest eggs. Insurance, medical bills, and cost of living are sky-high; my world although tolerable, is unstable. I love New Orleans, but I do not like the current living standards! I remember after the storm and all during my displacement, I'd run into folks who inevitably made reference to the notion that perhaps God had sent Katrina because New Orleans was such a sinful city. Although ill-fated activities were on the rise prior to the onset of Katrina, I would not allow myself to give in to those soothsayers' whispers that God was punishing New Orleans. However, now that I am home and see that the city has gotten more off track, I began to wonder whether or not there is any truth to the taunting. I am no politician, nor am I in leadership position; the very best I can do is pray and attempt to emulate Christ. I haven't given up on New Orleans because there are so many significant aspects to our existence. I have so many wonderful memories here. I am just prayerful that God, who spared us from the storm, continues to bless and protect us from all elements—including ourselves. We are very much in need of His embrace and guidance. I believe the overall objective of this book is to remind everyone to love one another; we all have problems and we are all human, but we are also all His children. If each one of us would volunteer to reject egos, we would probably be more susceptible to God's many blessings.

CHAPTER 8

DO YOU LIKE RETIREMENT?

Overall, yes, I am enjoying my retirement. It took time getting use to it, but in the end, I've learned to embrace it. I am not going to sit in judgment on anyone's decision to retire or whether to prolong the inevitable. I accept the general consensus that most folks are kind of brainwashed into thinking that if they're not working, they are not contributing members of society. I worked nearly forty-five years. Although I did not love all positions I held, I nonetheless liked the idea of earning my own finances. Being retired means I not only continued my own finances but I do not have to comply with a structured routine. I like that. I suppose my main objection to retirement is lack of camaraderie. Certainly, I still have friends but somehow it's different. I appreciate and enjoy the many who returned to New Orleans, yet I am also dealing with the loss of the many that did not come home. However, I've vowed not to become a nuisance. I use numerous forms of communication to remain in contact with family and friends. However, I do not demand or steal their time. I allow them to notify me when and if we are able to socialize. In the meantime, I find other interests to keep me occupied. I can definitely understand why some retired folks may feel the need to re-employ themselves, either with temporary or volunteer positions. And who knows, maybe one day I might find myself among those statistics. But for now, I am content.

CHAPTER 9

ARE YOU SATISFIED WITH THE REPAIRS TO YOUR HOME?

The aesthetic appeal of my repaired property is extremely eye-pleasing. The colors, both exterior and interior, are vibrant. The floor plan is significantly fluid; the crown molding and recessed lighting adds to its value. I have gotten many compliments and inquiries for the name of my contractor. Overall, I am pleased with the work. However, being me ... there are always some technicalities. Please keep in mind that those who are closest to me always seem to view my assessments with a grain of salt; they imply that I am a tad too picky. And most likely, they have a point. However, I can't help knowing what I like or speaking out against that which bothers me. In general, my contractor did a good job. However, in the long run and especially after discovering he was not licensed, I am not at all comfortable with the end results. Nevertheless, I do not complain or seek legal recourse. My living in Arkansas at the time of my contractual agreement did not allow much maneuverability on my part. I was in dire straits. I needed ... no, wanted desperately ... to have my home repaired. However, due to the tremendous influx of ruthless con artists and contracting scams which consumed the Gulf Coast communities, I was hesitant to hire anyone. These jackals knew exactly their vantage points. They preyed upon the desperate, elderly, and in general, the basic needs of storm victims. Everyone who owned property was vying and competing for contractual commitments. There was a supply and demand market that definitely gave contractors the edge. I would like to believe that there were some legitimate contractors willing to ply their trade without the use of fraud, neglect, or abuse. Unfortunately, the news that was reaching my ears was not very encouraging. The stories of rampant cons were viciously overwhelming. Insurance money as well as federal funds were being wrongfully invested on fast pitched schemes and sales artists. I was desperate, yet scared. I knew I had to swim in those shark-infested waters … that is, if I wanted my house repaired.

Utilizing the Internet to research contractual information was more of nuisance than a help. The businesses that were still operating in the devastated areas were considered blessings. However, that didn't mean that they were operating without criminal intent. And the businesses that flocked to the stricken area weren't necessarily all bad guys, either. The problem, therein the conflict, was the desperate demands. It did not take long for unscrupulous practices to inundate and victimize homeowners. And once the fraud began, the cycle of desperation increased.

Can you imagine having lost your home and personal belongings in a natural disaster only to become victim to money-hungry mongrels? What about attempting to reorganize your life so that you can regain some standard of living only to be waylaid by thieves and crooks? Moreover, once you begin the process of rebuilding, spending money allocated for that sole purpose, you find that not only your money is gone but your spirit as well is broken? How disheartening. I was terrified. I was reading tales of woe in the newspapers, listening to tears of exasperation from television interviews, and sharing personal experiences with my friends via telephone conversations. All was not good.

But again, I did not have a choice; this was my destiny. I

prayed without ceasing; I asked God to give me the courage and guidance needed so that I could get this necessity over and done. In addition, I asked Him to give me peace of mind once a decision had been made. I knew in the past, I'd given God burdens but then guiltily returned, taking back my cross and ultimately ending up wallowing in self-pity. Thankfully, the storm had taught me a lot; I was determined to give up this cross and allow Him to lead with me desperately following,

On that note, ironically on one of my visits to New Orleans, I came into contact with a reservist buddy, Sergeant Frederick. Frederick had returned to New Orleans and was in the process of having his home rebuilt. I shared with him my dilemma and concerns; he, in turn, put me in touch with the folks who were working for him. One of the guys associated with Frederick's contracting group was a relative of Frederick's. Because I believed that our paths had crossed due to a Godly intervention, I agreed to meet with his builders. Long story short, I contracted with these guys. I am not a carpenter and have no legal knowledge of their jargon. However, I knew what I desired and I really needed reliable resources. I felt that I had been drawn to my reservist friend, and since Frederick had a relative affiliated with these contractors, I concluded my prayers had been answered. Unfortunately, life is not all that simple. Maybe these were the guys for me, but halfway through the building process, I learned that these workers were sub-licensed. They knew how to do the work, but they were more or less glorified apprentices. I was disappointed; this meant that if anything went wrong, I would be engaged in a horrible game of finger-pointing. However, I felt it was too late to turn around. I'd had the peace of mind I asked for; thus, to do anything other than continue forward would create untold agony. So I increased my prayer rituals and home visits; I asked thousands of questions, shared my ideas, and sometimes made unexpected changes to their planned layout. Still, in the end, my home was finished satisfactorily. Moreover, after completion and with the use of a supplied overseer's license, city codes were met and my property passed inspection.

So why, you may ask, do I insist that my home is only aesthetically pleasing instead of overwhelmingly acceptable? I believe it's because now that I am actually living in the house, I get to see the numerous small imperfections daily. Thus far I have not observed any major flaws, but the ones that are visible are somewhat irritating. For instance, there are many door hanging errors—either the frames are off-kilter or the doors themselves are a smidge smaller than the frames. When I first moved in, I had to have Freon put in the AC unit; there were missing ducts and/or vents; and some of the plumbing lines needed adjustment. There are also some flooring errors. My floors are laminates and some of the slats are not tightly melded. In addition, my eyes are constantly drawn to cut-out spaces in the drywall that were not sufficiently measured. Moreover, there are pencil marks, paint splatters, and other oddities which constantly beckon my attention. However, so far everything, including the noticeable errors, are livable mistakes, yet because they exist and catch my attention daily, it gives me concerns about possible underlying undetected problems. No doubt, a licensed professional or better supervision could have enhanced the outcome of the work. Nonetheless, I keep reminding myself not to get worked up over cosmetics. Thus far, my home is comfortable; the few things requiring correction just have to be repaired in good time. That is, I've not discovered anything life threatening or completely inoperable, so I am convinced that my prayers were answered—my house is finished and my funds weren't misappropriated. I managed to keep raw nerves abated. Therefore, I am grateful for God's goodness!

CHAPTER **10**

HOW IS YOUR BOOK FARING?

My book is doing okay. By that I mean although it's nowhere near being on the bestseller list, it has some momentum. I am relatively an unknown. But that too is okay. I wrote my book to achieve a goal, to provide medical therapy, and to share personal encounters. I very much compare my quest of authoring to spotting a rainbow, chasing it, and being rewarded with a mystical pot of gold. In my case, however, the actual gold never materialized. Nevertheless, although my profit margin is less than dramatic, I am happy with my overall accomplishment. When I released my book, I never planned nor calculated huge monetary gains. I'm not saying that profits would not be desirous; only that it wasn't my primary motivation. My worst fears at that time were whether or not my story line and writing style had met its mark. It was like a mental measurement. I was concerned about the book's reception. I worried if my readers would be able to ascertain my train of thoughts. I wanted to ensure that what I was thinking and feeling in essence had been successfully translated. Once the book came out and feedback ensued, I was delighted. It didn't matter which emotions were being expressed, but rather that my work had some magnetism. In addition, I could not be more pleased that my journal made its way beyond Louisiana and Arkansas borders. Many readers who purchased my book came back to order additional copies for relatives and friends. Therefore, my book has been circulated and received in numerous households all over these United States. Moreover, since I maintain continued affiliation with my military friends, my book has even found its way abroad … Halleluiah!

My only overall drawback about publication is the marketing process. Most of my sales were made via word of mouth. I was also very fortunate to have had a few book signings. But sales are definitely not my forte. After the release of my book, I got a chance to pound pavement, lick stamps, as well as attempt personal sales. This, to me, is overwhelming, for although I possess some stage presence, I lack aggressiveness. And to be a newcomer in this particular field where salesmanship is a must, I am disadvantaged. Nevertheless, I am satisfied. I was able to document an event in my life, share that documentation with others, and receive adequate feedback concerning my endeavors.

CHAPTER 11

HAVE ANY SUGGESTIONS FOR OTHER FIRST TIME AUTHORS?

Primarily, I am indebted to all who had inquiries, suggestions, and encouragement about my book. If you too are interested in writing or having a book published, I offered this observation: Make sure the subject you chose is something which impacts you deeply. This way, once you begin the writing process, your ideas will flow. Moreover, go over your presentation repeatedly. Proofreading is a never ending process. I have often heard, "Words are peculiar; verbalization can easily be forgiven, but the written word can hunt you, forever."

Therefore, if you are a novice author and are leaning strongly toward releasing a book, go for it! But do so knowing your words, ideas, and presentation may be used as social measurement; some readers may offer kind reviews, some may react negatively, while others may intentionally be elusive. So be prepared. It's not very difficult to be thankful, but you may find yourself on a serious tightrope when and if you have to publicly defend your work. Thus far, my journey in life, to include the unfurling of Katrina, has helped me acquire thicker skin and a well-defined poker face. In addition, I am eternally grateful that the majority of my reviews were complimentary. The ones who responded negatively did so because of personal grievances, and the ones who intentionally withheld their comments, I chalked it up as testimony of a "job well done." As you can see, you can turn some negatives into triumphs.

In addition, please consider the following instincts or magnetism, which I believe produces a good story. Since the release of my first book, I've listened and fielded many inquiries from "would-be" authors. Mostly they have come from those who are either thinking about or who are actually writing their own stories. In several instances, I've even been asked to read raw manuscripts. I am amazed at the number of people who are actually interested in writing. I had been under the impression that with the introduction of Face book, texting, and other social networking, normal writing had become virtually extinct. I almost always preface my answers to these future authors with the following information: Writing has always been escapism for me. My family was very impoverished; we did not have a lot of materialistic belongings. Emphatically, we were dirt poor. Storytelling is a major part of my world. During my formative years, we were not privy to television or radio, nor did we subscribe to newspapers or magazines. Our main form of entertainment was storytelling. And miraculously, even as entertainment media found its way into our lives, the art of weaving the imagination into interesting tales remained.

As a child, I kept up with storytelling because it camouflaged hunger pains and the lack of basic requirements. As an adolescent I continued the escape because it amused me and mostly kept me out of trouble. As a young adult I wove stories because by then I was seriously addicted and the trips were relatively inexpensive. Even now, as a senior citizen, I continue to indulge myself; quite often I am up at night wandering in and out of imaginary worlds. I supposed it's safe to say I formulated my dreams and lifestyle based on fairy tale imagery. Although it has been speculated that writing skills are diminishing, I am still very much intrigued by it all. Once I discovered that I could lure and entertain others with my stories, words, and ideas, I myself was hooked! Although I am not an avid reader, I pride myself as being better than average.

The written adventure can be very captivating. When I find a novel or magazine article that holds my interest, I am immediately indisposed to other distractions. Moreover, I am often critical of others' presentations. I try to ascertain all possible outcomes prior to discovering the end results supplied by the author. I know this is may sound annoying, but to me it's challenging. Whether the format is a book or movie it does not matter; I am mesmerized by the art. I know the storyline is working when I find that I am actually involved with the thought process. In some instances, I've been known to profoundly change the conclusion of a presented work. I like when I find something that truly moves me … I cannot control my emotions. And that's what attracted me to authorship. I wanted to share that rollercoaster ride with others. Of course, I am speaking of social and entertaining scripts. I know that reports and other documentaries are a different genre and as such require different deliveries. As you probably suspect, the latter is not my calling.

My book, *In Search of Higher Grounds,* had all of the elements that I like. As I wrote it, I was so caught up in the suspense; it was almost as if I couldn't wait to see what happened next. Fortunately, the timeframe in which this book was written served multiple purposes. I advise the novice author to have purpose and a need to express. When you find that particular subject that ignites passion in your brain, creates energy within your spirit, and pulls you into an adventure, and then you are ready to compose. Don't let stumbling blocks thwart your efforts. There will be moments in your progression when you are stuck for ideas or translation. But don't give up. There is always a solution waiting to be exposed. I often use the tedious moments in my daily activities—such as trekking—to flush out hidden troves. You too will develop a power of release. This will give you a feeling of euphoria that far exceeds any mental anguish attempting to hold you prisoner.

Not long after the release of my book, I was overjoyed to view *The Bucket List,* a movie starring Jack Nicholson and Morgan Freeman. The premise of this movie captured my imagination and offered personal validation. By this, I mean that, although I had been getting good reviews for my book, I was also receiving mixed criticism. This whole reflective critique was new to me. In essence, I was an emotional wreck. I suppose one might deduce that perhaps I was not able to receive constructive criticism; thus, the overall negative feedback was deteriorating my confidence. I tried telling myself that my book was solid. I convinced myself that everyone would not have the same reception. Nonetheless, once you put your thoughts or ideas on paper for the entire world to scrutinize, you may be subjected to unflattering remarks. However after viewing *The Bucket List,* I got a little more of an appreciation for what I'd been able to accomplish. And once I'd attained that recertification, I was pumped! And the rest, as they say, is history.

I am not going to underestimate your capabilities. No doubt you probably understand that writing, publishing, and marketing a book can be mind boggling. It has its ups and downs. Yet if it is something you feel strongly about, conquer your fears and forge ahead. Moreover, I highly encourage interested authors to pen their ideas not just for publication but at every opportunity. Even if you have no interest in authoring a book, you can still find venues for your work. For many years, personal letters were my only chosen writing opportunities. But as time went on, I built up the courage to enter literary contests, write poems, and perform dramatic readings. I volunteered my services for plays, skits, and editorial presentations. Once you get the ideas flowing, allow the ink to splatter. Most importantly, don't be afraid to ask for help, and for heaven's sake, if you remember nothing else, read and re-read your output prior to release.

CHAPTER 12

THE END

Wow, I've reached an ending, or at least a point of closure! I hope to have answered your many inquiries, piqued your interest, and explored some of the continued controversies presented in my first journal. While structuring this book, I was mentally charged and eager for escapism. However, many of you may note that the completion of this book took longer than that of my first document. The delivery here was perhaps more tempered than expedient. I had a desire but not necessarily an express emergency. Fortunately, I had lots to share, so I used what I consider to be a natural rhythm. That is, my method of storytelling was neither haphazard nor hurried—just told as if in a conversation with my readers. I attempted to employ fluidity and added dates so that you could stay on track with the events as they were being described. I did this because everyday living consists of back and forth movements. I wanted to share with you my homecoming; I needed to catch you up and summarize my encounters in Arkansas; and I wanted you to know my present state of affairs. Therefore, I took my time; I thought about the information I wanted to include and proceeded to tell you about it as if we were just sitting and chatting. Overall, I wanted to make it detailed yet interesting.

In summation, being home and retired is both scary and rewarding. Although, as a community, Gulf Coast residents are severely handicapped by the lack of infrastructure, I still adore the idea of familiar grounds. I can find comfort here. Moreover, I am bound and determined to keep Jesus in my life. As I strived to harmonize my friends, memories, and finances, I embrace the spirit of Christ and the goodness of God.

When I started this book, Gulf Coast communities were besieged with grief regarding the BP oil spill; as I conclude my writing, the Mississippi River rising has our attention; moreover, as I push forward hoping for publication, hurricane season for 2011 has begun. Nonetheless, life continues. Trials and tribulations persist. However, God is good, and it is not my intent to wallow in the muck and mire created by mankind or nature. God has shown me love, and I hope to pass that message on to all willing to hear. In addition, He has gifted me with a form of communication. I hope to share that ability with those willing to read. And at the very least, I shall cling on to His unchanging Hand!

I love to write—the splattering of ink! Creative writing for me is mental and physical therapy. I marvel at the mind's ability to spill over onto paper and structure formative images that others are able to share, appreciate, and perhaps even enjoy. My God is awesome! I ended my last accounting by asserting that God was not through with me. I got a lot of interesting responses to that statement. Mostly, they were from folks wanting to know exactly what God was doing with me. I believe I have addressed most of those inquiries in this assessment. However, suffice it to say, as long as I draw breath, God will always be working on me. My trek through Hurricane Katrina, my brief residency in Arkansas, and now my reestablishment in New Orleans are just stepping stones. My overall premise is that I must continue to rely on and trust His word. I sometimes am guilty of rushing to fix things. I often jump to conclusions prior to consulting with Him. I know that I am human and subject to error, but He loves me anyway. As I continue to praise His Holy Name, I see the glass not as half empty or as half full. I instead view the container as Jesus and the substance provided, His grace, for which there is no measurement. His love endures forever!

THE END

Chapter 13

Afterword

I ended this manuscript and was in the midst of the process of schlepping publications when I could no longer bear my feelings that I'd been remiss. The time period inscribed herein either leads up to or encompasses the election of Barrack Obama, the forty-fourth president of these United States. Primarily, and because I do not want to be dismissed or ignored for lack of political awareness, I readily admit some deficiency concerning political astuteness. Nonetheless, I stand on my previous proclamation—I know what I like! Moreover, the election and subsequent assignment of Barrack Obama to the office of US president is by far the most historic event occurring in my lifetime. Therefore, exclusion of this prestigious benchmark would be unforgiveable.

While in Arkansas, the election process went on seemingly

without significant disorder. At least, there was nothing that forewarned of regression. Absolutely, there was some disgruntled feeling, but for the most part, common sense prevailed. Nonetheless, in my adopted community, I was caught off guard. I wasn't prepared for all the disrupting fanfare occurring after the election. Might I point out, the overall dissension was not restricted only to Arkansas. Citizens all across this great nation contributed to the mayhem and distraction preceding and proceeding Obama's inauguration. I suppose my particular naivety may have been spearheaded by misconception. The Arkansas community where I resided was not very forthright; everyone from civic to spiritual leaders hawked the power of prayers. In my mind and heart, I perceived their message to mean that they were praying for a leadership that would solidify the nation and pull this country up by the bootstraps. From the pulpit, I heard, "We must pray without ceasing for a leader who will be able to guide this nation into the twenty-second century." From the communities, I heard, "We must all do our part to ensure America is a continuing force to be reckoned with. However, once Obama was elected, my short lived sense of pride and arrival greatly diminished. Immediately after the election the insanity revealed itself. It was as though the whole country had been in a hypnotic trance and had suddenly waken up; although opponents wanted to proclaim righteousness, no one wanted to abide by the majority rule application of our nation. Many whites along with small groups of minorities became viciously and verbally abusive. "They" began to question all aspects as pertained to Barrack

Obama. Was his election official? Was recourse possible? Were they really expected to respect his leadership? Who voted him in? Is he a natural citizen? What is his educational background? They questioned his military record and family history. Were there legalities which would allow impeachment/annulment? In other words ... "Do Over!"

I was stunned! The extent to which many whites as well as other vigilantes sought to minimize, denigrate, and disrespect the highest office of our land was shameful! I am still awed. I am back in my hometown, yet the controversy continues. There's been so much trash talking, name calling, and acts of defiance, I fear for our nation's future. Nevertheless, in my opinion, Barack Obama has not faltered. He appears to know his mission; moreover, and what is most important, he seems very familiar with the opposition. I further believe that he has handled his office with dignity, knowledge, and grace. Unfortunately, negative public opinion and the lack of congressional support have reduced his office to that of a lame duck administration. Of course I am saddened by this outcome. I pray for him as well as our nation. This ignorance sets us back tremendously. If all the foolishness persists based on liberal remorse, then our political system has failed and in its place is anarchy!

I beseech God's blessings and empowerment. As a formidable world power, this nation should not be so obsessed and concerned with the sifting of its citizens. Heavenly Father teach us to let go and to let God; Give us the strength and courage to love one another in the same manner which you love us. Teach us not to cower behind rags of righteousness but rather that there is room at the cross for all.

"I'm so glad that trouble don't last all ways." I am not sure who coined that adage or why; it has been my experience that "trouble," although subject to brief pause, is never ending. These days, I am more inclined to simply be thankful for blessings received. For although troubles seemingly outnumber blessings, the latter, no doubt, are more enduring. I believe the twenty-third Psalm gives credence to my summation: "Yea, though I walk through the valley of the shadow of death ..." This very familiar quote is reminiscent of life's constant struggles. As a child, I always associated this biblical verse with comfort for the loved ones of the deceased. As I grew older, I began to understand the verse to mean that the deceased had entered the valley and that relatives should not mourn their loss because God is at the helm. But now, as I myself am being overshadowed, I realize that this verse covers all—that is, our survival is very much dependent on Him. Without God, we walk in darkness; with Him, we have an inkling of light and therefore, Grace, "For whosoever believes in Him shall not perish ..." If I had to compare my troubles to blessings received, no doubt I'd be overwhelmed. Nonetheless, I believe that trouble is God's way of reminding us that without Him, we are lost, that this Earthly existence is short and our deeds are costly. We suffer more here because this is not our ultimate existence. Yea, we remember the hurt, pain, and disappointments. We also rejoice in the breath of relief, the exuberance of life, or the release of tension when blessings are received, so much so that we often forget about the intensity of trouble.

No doubt folks can identify trouble; that is, we recognize when we are surrounded by it, but quite often we cannot sincerely express the magnitude of gratification experienced when that light at the end of the tunnel appears. Hopefully, this book will give you an idea of that imagery. I remember my past as I live in the present. Moreover, I am basking in and sharing his goodness daily. When I started this second attempt at publication it was mid-2010; I am home, back in New Orleans, and living in my repaired home. As I end this book, Ink Splatters, it is mid-2011, and I remain born of His Spirit, washed in His Blood!